Suppliers

Craft Creations Ltd
Ingersoll House
Delamare Road
Cheshunt EN8 9ND
Tel: 01992 781900
Mail order service
(Paper manufacturers: card blanks, mounting card)

Craft World (Head office only)
No 8 North Street, Guildford
Surrey GU1 4AF
Tel: 07000 757070
Retail shops nationwide, telephone for local store
(Craft Warehouse)

D M C Creative World Ltd
Pullman Road, Wigston
Leicestershire LE8 2DY
Tel: 0116 281 1040
Telephone or write for your nearest retail stockist
(Aida fabric and napkins)

Dylon International Ltd (Head office only)
Worsley Bridge Road
London SE26 5HD
Tel: 0181 663 4295
Telephone for your local retail stockist
(Fabric Paint)

Habitat UK
196 Tottenham Court Road
London W1P 9LD
Tel: 0645 334433
Retail shops nationwide, telephone for local store
(Hessian rugs)

Hobby Crafts (Head office only)
River Court
Southern Sector
Bournemouth International Airport
Christchurch
Dorset BH23 6SE
Tel: 0800 272387 freephone
Retail shops nationwide, telephone for local store
(Craft Warehouse)

Home Crafts Direct
PO Box 38
Leicester LE1 9BU
Tel: 0116 251 3139
Mail order service
(Stencil card, film, tools and equipment)

Humbrol Ltd (Head office only)
Marfleet
Hull HU9 5NE
Tel: 01482 701191
Telephone for your local retail stockist
(Enamel paint manufacturer)

Lakeland Ltd
Alexandra Buildings, Windermere
Cumbria LA23 1BQ
Tel: 01539 488100
Retail shops nationwide and a mail order service
(Wooden breadboard and kitchen products)

Offray & Son Ltd (Head office only)
Fir Tree Place, Church Road
Ashford
Middlesex TW15 2PH
Tel: 01784 247281
Telephone for your local retail stockist
(Ribbon manufacturer)

Scumble Goosie
Lewiston Mill, Toadsmoor Road
Stroud
Gloucestershire GL5 2TB
Tel: 01453 731305
Mail order service
(Wooden blanks for stencilling, paint and varnish)

Squires Model & Craft Tools
The Old Corn Store
Chessels Farm, Hoe Lane
Bognor Regis
West Sussex PO22 8NW
Tel: 01243 587009
Mail order service
(Craft Tools)

Stencilling
made easy

Series Editors: Susan & Martin Penny

David & Charles

A DAVID & CHARLES BOOK

First published in the UK in 1998

A catalogue record for this book is available from the British Library.

ISBN 0 7153 0562 X

Series Editors: Susan & Martin Penny
Designed by Penny & Penny
Illustrations: Fred Fieber at Red Crayola
Photography: Ashton James; Jon Stone
Stylist: Susan Penny

Printed in France by Imprimerie Pollina S. A.
for David & Charles
Brunel House Newton Abbot Devon

Contents

✻ ✻ ✻ ✻ ✻ ✻ ✻

Introduction to Stencilling

Stencilling Made Easy is a complete guide to the craft of stencilling; we take you through the mysteries of which equipment to buy; give you hints on preparation, and the skills needed to cut stencils. By following the step-by-step instructions, you will quickly learn the essential techniques needed to create your own exciting projects

Making stencils

Below is a list of the essential equipment needed to cut stencils:

- **Stencil card** – thick yellow card, soaked in linseed oil to make it waterproof and pliable.
- **Acetate and stencil film** – a pliable clear plastic which can be drawn directly on to, and will show the design from below.
- **Cork** – pliable thin cork or a cork tile. Good for stencilling on fabric.
- **Paper** – use copier paper to trace or photocopy the design; useful when making masks for reverse stencilling.
- **Typewriter carbon paper** – use for transferring a tracing to stencil card.
- **Cutting mat** – a mat that self heals when cut and will protect your work surface.
- **Cutting knife** – slim, very sharp craft knife used for cutting stencil card or acetate.
- **Fine sandpaper** – use decorator's sandpaper for rubbing down wooden surfaces, and removing snags from the underside of stencils.

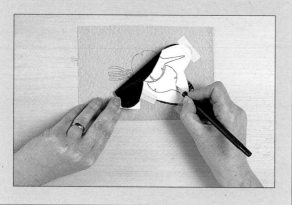

Painting with stencils

Below is a list of the essential equipment needed for painting stencil designs:

- **Stencil brush** – a stiff bristled brush with a flat top, made in different sizes and thicknesses.
- **Sponge** – use a natural sea sponge for a soft paint effect; or a synthetic sponge, cut from a kitchen scourer for a more textured effect.
- **Artist's paintbrush** – use to add highlights to a wet or dry stencilled design; or fine lines to flower stems or leaf veins.
- **Decorator's paintbrush** – use to apply a wash or base coat to wood; or to add a coat of varnish.
- **Dish for mixing paint** – use a plastic microwave dish, fresh food tray or tin foil dish; or a small artist's palette.
- **Kitchen paper** – useful for removing excess paint from a brush, mopping up spills and cleaning brushes.
- **Cotton buds** – used to clean stencils.
- **Cocktail stick** – used for mixing paint.

Tips for stencilling on tiles

✔ Use terracotta or unsealed floor tiles
✔ Seal the surface with matt emulsion paint
✔ Use acrylic paints on tiles, as they have the brightest colour range
✔ Apply the paint using a sponge
✔ Seal the stencilled tile with acrylic varnish
✔ Only use stencilled tiles in low wear areas

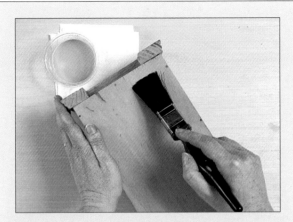

Tips for stencilling on wood

- ✔ Rub down the wood using fine sandpaper
- ✔ Colour the surface of bare wood with a wash
- ✔ Use spray adhesive to mount the stencil
- ✔ Seal the stencilled wood with acrylic varnish

Tips for stencilling on metal

- ✔ Rub down with wet and dry sandpaper
- ✔ Use a spray primer to seal the bare metal
- ✔ Allow to dry before removing the stencil
- ✔ Seal the surface with polyurethane varnish

Tips for stencilling on paper

- ✔ Use uncoated paper
- ✔ Do not overload the paper with paint
- ✔ Spray paint will give the best finish
- ✔ Doilies make good masks for stencilling
- ✔ Leave the stencilled paper to dry flat

Tips for stencilling on fabric

- ✔ Use calico or cotton based fabric
- ✔ Wash to remove 'finishing' and shrinkage
- ✔ Test the paint on the fabric, for bleeding
- ✔ Fix fabric paint with an iron before washing
- ✔ Use fabric paint for most fabrics; emulsion paint can be used on stiff fabric like hessian
- ✔ Seal emulsion with a PVA glue/water mix

Choosing the right paint

Choosing the right paint for the right surface can be difficult: listed below are some of the plus and minus points to help you make that choice.

- **Stencil paint** – Water-based
    - The right consistency for stencilling
    - Colours can be mixed
    - Will give good results on most surfaces
    - Brushes can be washed in water
    - Use water-based varnish to seal
    - Very expensive compared with acrylics
- **Acrylic** – Water-based
    - The right consistency for stencilling
    - Colours can be mixed
    - Large range of colours available
    - Will give good results on most surfaces
    - Brushes can be washed in water
    - Dries fast, may need a 'retarder'
    - Use water-based varnish to seal
- **Emulsion** – Water-based
    - Sold in small tester pots
    - Mostly pale colours, but can be mixed
    - Too slow to dry for most projects
    - Paint thin, but works well on fabric
- **Fabric paint** – Water-based
    - Some makes too thin for stencilling
    - Colours can be mixed
    - Test for 'bleeding'
    - Brushes can be washed in water
    - Iron fix before laundering
- **Enamel paint** – Oil-based
    - Use on metal surfaces
    - Brushes must be cleaned in white spirit
    - Work in a well ventilated room
- **Spray paint** – Most are cellulose based
    - Must be stored at room temperature
    - Use in a well ventilated room
    - Shake well, spray from 30-46cm (12-18in)
- **Matt acrylic varnish** – Water-based
    - Brush and spray-on
    - Wash brushes in water
    - No smell and dries very quickly
- **Polyurethane varnish** – Oil-based
    - Brush-on, very slow to dry
    - Wash brushes in white spirit
    - Work in a well ventilated room

Making Stencils

A stencil can be cut from almost any flat material: card, acetate, clear film, cork or paper. How you make a stencil and what you make it from depends on the craft materials that are available to you. The recommended method of working is given within each project, but you may prefer to try a different technique

Using carbon paper

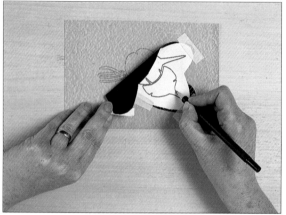

To transfer the design to stencil card, place typewriter carbon paper between the card and the tracing. Draw over the lines firmly using a ball-point pen.

Cutting a stencil

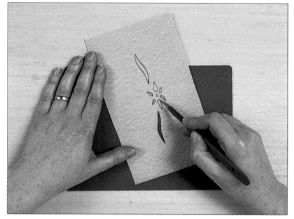

Hold the uncut stencil on a cutting mat and following the design lines, start cutting from the centre. Move the stencil as you cut, drawing the knife towards you.

Using acetate

To transfer the design to clear acetate or stencil film, place a tracing of the design under the acetate or film then draw over the lines firmly using a felt-tipped pen.

Rubbing down

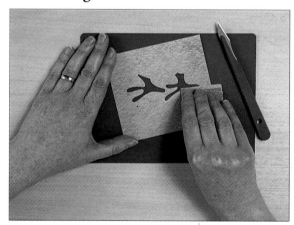

After cutting the stencil, check the underside for snags – these should be removed using fine sandpaper, to ensure the stencil will fit snugly when attached to the prepared surface.

Mounting a stencil

Lay the stencil face down on paper. Working in a well ventilated room, coat the back with spray mount adhesive – this will keep the stencil flat while painting, but can easily be removed with white spirit. Position the stencil on the prepared painting surface, holding in place with masking tape.

Repairing a stencil

To repair a stencil if you make a mistake whilst cutting or it gets broken while in use: clean around the area to be mended, then lay the stencil on a cutting mat covering the break with sticky tape. Turn the stencil over and repeat on the other side. Cut away the excess tape using a sharp craft knife.

Making a leaf stencil

To make a stencil from a leaf or flat object: attach the leaf or object to a thin cork sheet using sticky tape. Draw around the shape with a felt-tipped pen. Place the cork on a cutting mat and, using a sharp craft knife or small scissors, cut around the drawn shape, neatening any points or corners.

Using a cookie cutter

To scribble stencil on to fabric: position a cookie cutter on to the prepared fabric, holding firmly with one hand. Using a fabric painting felt pen and starting at the top, scribble from side to side within the cutter, touching each side as you move down towards the bottom of the shape.

Painting Techniques

Traditionally stencil paint is applied using a flat-ended brush, but you may want to try another method of applying the paint. A sponge dipped in paint and dabbed on to the surface will give a mottled folk art look; or you could try using spray paint to give a finer, more even paint finish

Loading the brush

Load the stencil brush with paint, then dab on to kitchen paper to remove the excess paint, giving an almost dry brush. Do this each time you add paint to the brush.

Adding highlights

To highlight the design: using a small stencil brush, dab paint on to the wet or dry stencilled design, at the edges or the centre to give a three-dimensional effect.

Pouncing

Using a loaded stencil brush, apply paint to the parts of the design not covered by the stencil. Use a soft pouncing or gentle circular movement with the brush.

Sponging

Dip a piece of sponge into the paint. Dab the sponge on to the design area not covered by the stencil. Apply the paint lightly to create a mottled effect.

Using a doily

In a well ventilated room, lightly coat the back of a doily with spray mount adhesive, then position right side up on a sheet of paper. Shake the paint can, then holding upright, spray the doily and the paper between, from a distance of 30-46cm (12-18in). Remove the doily, leave to dry.

Reverse stencilling

Stretch the material on to card, then mask off the areas not to be painted: use paper shapes attached with tape or torn masking tape strips. Using a large stencil brush, dab fabric paint on to the material, building up the colour slowly. Leave to dry, then remove the paper shapes. To fix the paint, see page 12.

Cleaning a stencil

Keep the stencil free from paint by cleaning both sides between applications. Use kitchen paper and a cotton bud dipped in water to remove water based paint; for oil based paint use white spirit. Good adhesion to the surface will stop the paint 'bleeding' behind the stencil.

Washing brushes

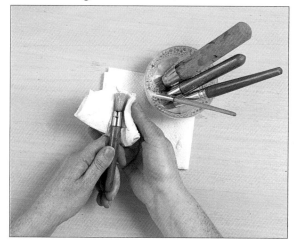

Wash brushes in warm soapy water at regular intervals while in use, and when changing paint colour – this will stop a build-up of paint. Clean and dry the brushes thoroughly before storing upright. A rubber band wrapped around the bristles will help keep them in good condition.

Painting on Fabric

Stencilling on fabric requires extra care in preparation and finishing: fabric should be washed to remove the 'finishing', then ironed on a fluffy towel. For fabric that cannot be laundered, coat with a mix of PVA glue and water. This will seal the surface, protecting it from dirt

Preparing fabric

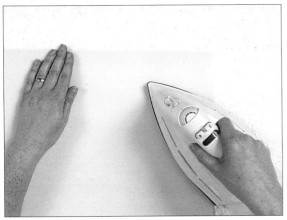

Fabric should be laundered before applying paint to remove the 'finishing' and take-up any shrinkage in the fabric: wash in warm soapy water, then iron on a fluffy towel.

Fixing fabric paint

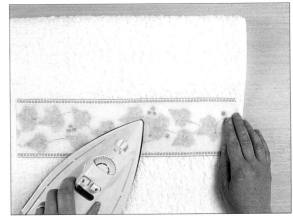

Stencilled fabric should be heat fixed to stop the paint washing out. Place the dry fabric face down on a towel. Iron for 1-2 minutes on the hottest setting suitable for the fabric.

Using fabric paint

Working with an almost dry brush, pounce paint within the design area of the stencil. Remove the stencil, clean, then reposition on the fabric. To fix the paint, see above.

Sealing surfaces

To protect fabric that is difficult to launder: coat with PVA glue mixed with an equal quantity of water, working the mix into the weave of the fabric. Dry flat for several days.

Hints and Tips

Some surfaces will require a little more preparation work than others. If you are working on wood, you may want to colour the background; on tiles the surface will need sealing. Here you will find useful advice that will speed up the work, leaving more time for the stencilling

Masking tape guides

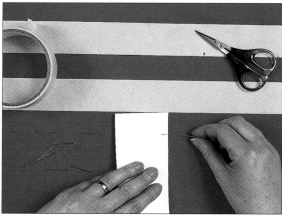

When stencilling in rows on fabric: make a paper marker just larger than the width of the design. Use pins to mark rows across the fabric. Stick masking tape along the rows.

Applying a wash to wood

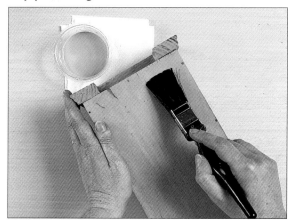

To colour a wooden surface before stencilling: lightly sand the wood, then wipe with a damp cloth. Mix emulsion paint with water, then paint the wood, leaving to dry overnight.

Covering a mistake

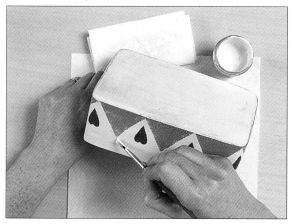

To remove stencil paint that has spread on to the background: sand the mark carefully, then wipe clean using a damp cloth. Repaint the area with the background colour.

Stencilling on tiles

Paint quarry or unsealed tiles with three coats of emulsion paint, before you begin stencilling. After stencilling, seal the tile with several coats of matt acrylic varnish.

Barge Roses Garden Set

Create a traditional hand-painted look for your garden accessories with these barge-painting designs. It's easy to picture this watering can on the roof of a canal boat, and the window box and terracotta pot adorning the lock-keeper's cottage. Why not use stencils to create this charming style?

You will need

- Wooden window box
- Metal watering can
- Terracotta pot
- Matt emulsion (tester pot size) – yellow, red, blue, white, pale green, dark green
- Gloss enamel paints – emerald green, dark green, bright red, white, yellow
- Metal primer, wood primer, clear polyurethane varnish, matt acrylic varnish
- Sandpaper – wet and dry
- Stencil card, film or acetate
- Typewriter carbon paper, white paper, two A4 sheets tracing paper
- Ball-point pen, soft pencil, chalk
- Large and medium stencil brush
- Decorator's paint brush
- Craft knife, cutting mat, ruler
- Masking tape, spray mount adhesive
- Cocktail sticks, flat dish for mixing paint, kitchen paper, newspaper, white spirit

Tracing the design

1 Trace over the two floral designs on pages 18 and 19 on to white paper with a soft pencil. Alternatively trace directly on to stencil film or acetate (see Making Stencils, page 8).

2 If you are using stencil card, cut a piece 5cm (2in) larger than each tracing, and cut the carbon paper to the same size. Lay the stencil card on a flat surface and secure with masking tape. Lay the carbon on top, inked side facing down. Over this, lay the tracing, and fix securely with masking tape. Carefully go over the design lines with a ball-point pen, pressing hard enough to ensure a good transfer. Repeat for the other design.

Cutting the stencil

1 Place the stencil card, film or acetate on a cutting mat and hold with one hand. Using a sharp craft knife, and following the design lines, start cutting from the centre of the design – this will ensure the stencil structure stays firm. Move the stencil around as you cut, drawing the knife towards you.

2 If you make a mistake and cut incorrectly, repair the stencil with sticky tape, then cut away any excess tape with a sharp knife. After the stencil has been cut, check the underside for snags – these should be removed carefully with fine sandpaper.

Preparing the window box

1 Smooth down any rough surfaces on your window box with sandpaper before applying one coat of wood primer. Allow to dry.

2 Using emulsion, paint two coats on the front, back and sides of the window box. Pick out any decorative features such as a scalloped top in yellow.

Positioning the stencil

1 Lay the stencil face down on a piece of newspaper. Finely coat the back of the stencil with spray mount adhesive: the adhesive will hold the stencil firmly while painting the design, but can easily be removed with a little white spirit.

2 Position the stencil on the project, holding firmly in place with small pieces of masking tape. To position the stencil on the window box, use a ruler and chalk; if your box is wider than the project example, you may be able to fit three or more repeat patterns along the front and back. In which case, position and paint the central design first, then re-position the stencil working outwards.

3 When positioning the second stencil make sure that it is the same height and distance from the sides and the top. The project example shows both roses and daisies stencils also being used in reverse. If you wish to do this clean and dry the stencil before turning it over.

Painting the window box

1 Using a stencil brush apply paint in a soft pouncing, circular movement to the flowers and the leaves. Use a clean brush for each colour and do not overload with paint. The roses are painted white, yellow and red with yellow detail and green leaves; the daisies are white with yellow and blue detail. When dry

apply highlights in toning colours. Allow to dry completely before removing the stencil.

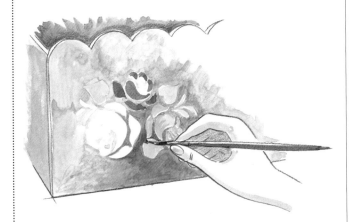

2 If any bleeding has occurred on to the background, touch-up with a fine brush using the appropriate background colour.

Painting the flower pot

1 Paint the outside of the flower pot with a coat of wood primer, to seal the porous surface of the pot; leave to dry. Paint the outside of the pot with a coat of red emulsion paint and the rim yellow.

2 Position the daisy stencil on to the front of the pot, and hold in place with small pieces of masking tape. Apply paint to the design using the same colours as the window box. Allow to dry before removing the stencil.

Painting the watering can

1 If you are using an old metal watering can, smooth down any rough surfaces using wet and dry sandpaper.

2 Wipe over the surface with a damp cloth to remove any dust, then apply one coat of metal primer to the outside of the can. Allow to dry.

3 Enamel paints should be used for painting metal or enamel surfaces. Brushes will need cleaning in white spirit. Cover your working surface with newspaper and wear gloves to protect your hands. Stir each colour thoroughly, before you begin. Enamel paint dries slowly so mistakes can be wiped away with a little white spirit on a cloth.

4 Paint the body of the watering can in dark green. Allow to dry. Secure the rose stencil to the side of the can. Using a stencil brush, apply paint to the design using the same colours as the window box. Allow to dry completely before removing the stencil.

Sealing the surfaces

1 The window box should be sealed inside and out with two or three coats of matt acrylic varnish: this will help to protect it from dust and knocks; drill holes through the bottom to let water drain through; and if possible put your plants into pots before placing them inside the box. The flower pot should be sealed in the same way.

2 To seal the outer surface of the watering can, paint with two or three coats of polyurethane varnish.

Use these two designs to create your own
barge-style stencils.

Scribble Bag and Box

Here's a really quick way to create a stencilled look. Use any simple shape as a 'stencil' and scribble the design with a fabric felt pen. Cookie cutters are just right and come in a variety of shapes and sizes. This is an ideal project for the stencilling beginner, giving a very satisfying fast finish

Wash the calico fabric in warm soapy water before you begin painting. This will remove any 'finishing' that may have been applied to the fabric and so stop the paint adhering to the surface of the fabric.

NOTE The eyelets will be sold with their own tool for punching through the fabric.

You will need

- Calico 46cm (½yd) x 90cm (36in) wide, plus enough to cover the shoe box
- Cotton gingham (½yd) 46cm x 90cm (36in) wide – green
- Ribbon 2cm (¾in) wide x 2m (2¼yd) – green
- Grosgrain ribbon, 2cm (¾in) wide – for box lid
- Twelve 11mm (⅜in) diameter eyelets
- Cookie cutters – leaf, flower, star and heart
- Fabric paint felt pens – green, red, blue, mauve
- Cardboard shoe box
- Sewing machine, sewing thread, scissors
- All-purpose glue, masking tape
- Iron, white cotton cloth

Scribbling on the bag

1 Cut two rectangles of calico and two of gingham 38x35.5cm (15x14in). If you do not have shaped cookie cutters, make stencils of the shapes on page 23 (see Making Stencils, page 8).

2 Position the leaf cookie cutter or stencil centrally on one calico rectangle 6cm (2⅜in) above the lower short edge of the fabric. If using a stencil, hold in place with small pieces of masking tape.

3 Using a green fabric painting felt pen, scribble within the shape, working slowly from side to side and moving down towards the bottom of the leaf. Remove the cutter or stencil from the fabric. Re-position to one side of the first stencilled leaf, scribble within the shape, then move and repeat on the other side of the central leaf.

4 Leave the paint to dry for thirty minutes then fix, following the manufacturer's instructions. This is done by placing a soft cloth over the painted area and pressing with a warm iron to set the paint on the fabric.

Making up the bag

1 Place the two rectangles of calico right sides together. Stitch taking a 1.5cm (⅝in) seam allowance around three sides, leaving the short

top edge open. Repeat for the gingham rectangles. Press the seams open.

2 With right sides facing, slip one bag inside the other. Stitch the bags together along the upper edge, leaving a gap for turning.

3 Turn right side out through the gap in the top seam. Close the gap in the top seam using small neat stitches.

4 Attach the twelve eyelets, equal distance apart, 5.5cm (2¼in) below the upper edge of the bag.

5 Cut the ribbon in half. Starting at one side of the bag, thread one length of ribbon

through the eyelet holes. Thread the other ribbon through the holes starting at the opposite side. Knot the ends together.

Preparing the box

1 Cut a strip of calico the distance around the box plus 2.5cm (1in) and the depth plus 4cm (1½in).

2 Cut a rectangle of calico to fit over the lid and lid sides adding 2cm (¾in) to all edges.

Scribbling on the box

1 Position the cookie cutter or the stencil on the calico cut for the box sides. Work within the area of calico that will cover the box sides. Scribble within the shapes using the

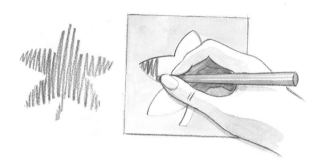

fabric painting felt pens. Leave to dry for thirty minutes, then fix the paint with a warm iron.

Covering the box

1 Spread glue evenly on one side of the box, press on the painted calico strip with 1.5cm (⅝in) extending beyond one end of the box and 2cm (¾in) extending above and below. Smooth the fabric outwards from the centre. Continue sticking the strip around the box sides; when you reach the last side, glue the extended fabric end to the box, before turning under the last raw edge and gluing in place.

2 Snip the lower edge of the fabric up to each corner. Fold the extra fabric at the bottom of the box over on to the bottom and glue to the base. Snip the upper edge in the same way, fold inside the box then glue in place. Glue a length of grosgrain ribbon inside the box, covering the raw edges.

3 Spread glue on the lid of the box, press the calico rectangle centrally on top, smoothing the fabric out towards the corners. Snip the corners then glue the fabric to the rim of the box lid, trimming any excess fabric at the corners. Glue grosgrain ribbon to the rim of the box lid, lining it up with the lower edge of the lid.

Use these shapes to make stencils if you do not have cookie cutters.

Lacy Wrapping and Cards

If you don't have time to make a gift yourself, making the wrapping paper is the next best thing. It's not just an economical way to make gift-wrap, but also fun and easy to do. Dressed up with metallic ribbon your gift will be the tops – even before it's opened!

To make wrap for other gift giving occasions, use different colours of paper and spray paint: try primary coloured paint on white paper for fun birthday wrapping or white on silver for a wedding gift.

You will need

- Paper for stencilling – white, cream, gold
- Card for making greetings cards and tags – white, gold
- Luggage tags – white
- Gift box - plain white, cream, gold
- Paper doilies
- Spray mount adhesive
- Lighter fuel and cotton buds – for cleaning off the glue
- Spray paint – copper, gold
- Ribbon – copper, gold
- Cabochon jewellery stones
- White tracing paper, soft pencil
- All-purpose glue, newspaper, scissors

Stencilling with the doily

1 Cover your work surface with lots of newspaper or scrap paper. When using spray adhesive or spray paint, always work in a well ventilated room.

2 Lightly spray the back of a doily with spray mount adhesive. Position the doily right side up on a sheet of paper. Continue adding doilies to the paper in this way, either overlapping the edges or positioning close together, until the paper is covered. The adhesive will stop the doily from moving in the breeze from the spray paint.

3 Spray paint should be stored at room temperature, shake well before using. Hold the can upright and spray from a distance of 30-46cm (12-18in) from the paper. Spray the doily and the paper between evenly (see Using a Doily, page 11). Leave for a few seconds, then carefully peel off the doilies. Leave to dry.

4 If the spray adhesive has made the stencilled paper sticky, dab it away carefully using lighter fuel on a cotton bud, do not rub the paper or the paint may smudge.

5 Use the stencilled paper to gift wrap presents and cover gift boxes; or you may prefer, if you have a plain card gift box, to stencil directly on to the surface of the box.

Tie with sheer bronze or gold ribbon and label with luggage tags that have been stencilled in the same way as the paper, or make your own from white card (see page 27).

Making the jewelled cards

1 Trace over the crown and star shape on page 27 on to white paper with a soft pencil. Carefully cut out the shapes from the paper. Hold the cut shapes on to the doily stencilled paper and draw around the outside edge with the pencil. Remove the shapes and cut around the pencil line.

2 Cut a rectangle of gold card 25x17cm (10x6½in) and a rectangle of white card 25x12.5cm (10x5in). Score centrally across the width of the cards and fold in half along the scored lines.

3 Stick the crown centrally to the front of the gold card and the star centrally to the front of the white card. Glue jewellery stones to the points of the crown and centre of the star.

Making a stencilled tag

1 To make a stencilled tag, trace off the tag shape at the bottom of this page, then draw the shape on to the white card. Cover with part of a doily, then spray with the gold or copper paint. When making tags it will save time and paper if you trace several on to the paper before spraying. Make a hole in the top of the tag and thread with ribbon.

Making a stencilled gift box

1 Lightly spray the back of a doily with spray mount adhesive, then wrap it around one corner of the gift box. Cut away any doily that is not stuck to the box. Continue adding doilies close together, but not overlapping, until the box is covered. To cover the lid, position a single doily on top, wrapping it down over the sides.

2 Spray with the gold or copper paint. Leave for a few seconds, then carefully peel off the doilies. Leave to dry then decorate with ribbon and a matching tag.

Use these shapes to make cards and gift tags.

Farmyard Tiles

Decorate country style! These charming animal tiles look great when used to co-ordinate a room. Stencil on your kitchen cupboard; or use porcelain paint to stencil on to china. With just a change of colour you can match the tiles to your curtains and table linen; or you could stencil those as well

The stencils used for this project have been cut from white copier paper. For each design you will have to cut several different masks to paint the individual colours on the tile. You will have to cut a new set of masks for each tile you want to paint.

You will need

- Terracotta floor tiles
- Matt emulsion paint – terracotta
- Matt acrylic varnish
- Acrylic paints – blue, green, white, black, yellow, rust red
- Decorator's brush
- Sponge pieces cut from a kitchen scourer
- White copier paper, soft pencil, masking tape
- Small sharp scissors, tape measure, masking tape
- Flat dish for mixing paint, container of clean water, kitchen paper

Cutting the stencils

1 Trace the designs on pages 30 and 31, on to white copier paper to make individual masks for the tiles. For each tile you will need a small square to paint the border; a larger square with the four corner hearts and wavy border lines; the large square with a full animal shape, and two opposite hearts for position; and a large square with the detail for each animal with two opposite hearts for position. Use the diagrams on page 31 for cutting and organising the masks.

2 Cut out the paper masks using small sharp scissors.

Painting the tiles

1 Using the flat decorator's brush, paint three or more coats of terracotta emulsion paint on the surface and side edges of the tiles. Leave to dry overnight.

2 Fix the small square paper mask on the surface of the tile with pieces of masking tape. Use a tape measure to position the paper in the centre of the tile.

3 Pour blue acrylic paint into a flat dish. Pick up the paint on a piece of sponge. Dab around the paper mask on the outer edges of the tile – do not completely cover the base paint. Remove the mask. Leave to dry.

29

4 Position the large square mask on the tile. Using a piece of sponge and the green paint, sponge the four wavy border lines and the four hearts. Carefully remove the mask, leave to dry.

5 Position the large square mask with the cut-out animal shape on the tile – use the hearts to position the mask in the correct place. With white paint, sponge the animal body. Remove the mask, leave to dry.

6 Lay the detail mask on the tile, again using the hearts to help with the position. Sponge black spots, ears, eyes, nose, tail end and a red

udder for the cow; red ears, eye, tail for the pig; black legs, ears, nose and eye for the sheep; for the goose a yellow beak, feet and eye.

7 Using an almost dry sponge, add highlights to the body of the animals; red for the underbelly of the pig; black over the sheep wool; and for the goose, cut a mask of the wing, position on his side, then sponge in yellow around the edge.

8 Leave the tiles to dry, then paint with at least three coats of matt acrylic varnish. Leave to dry thoroughly before fixing to the wall. Although the tiles have been sealed and can be wiped clean, they should not be used in areas where they will receive heavy wear, or if they need to be scrubbed to remove surface dirt.

When making the masks use the crosses above and below the animals to line-up with the crosses on the main mask. Cut the goose wing as a separate mask.

Use these diagrams to make individual masks for each stencil colour. Cut a set for each animal, using the large crosses to position the animals correctly.

Blue sponging mask

Green hearts and border

White animals' bodies

Detail stencilling: animal features

Cat T-shirt and Sneakers

Traditional stencilling is usually done inside a shape: for these contrary cats everything is reversed! The cut-out shapes are placed and painted around, leaving the cats' heads white. Create a different look by changing the background colour or eye shape, making yourself a whole new wardrobe!

Any cotton T-shirt can be used to complete this project, although white will give more impact to the cats' faces, other combinations of paint colours will give very different effects: black and silver would look very dramatic whereas brown and black would give a jungle print feeling.

You will need

- T-shirt – white cotton
- Sneakers – white canvas
- Fabric paint – red, royal blue, black, white, yellow, silver
- White paper, white card, soft pencil
- Craft knife, cutting mat, scissors, masking tape, double sided tape, tissue paper
- Large and small stencil brush, watercolour brush
- Flat dish for mixing paint
- Iron, white cotton cloth

Tracing the design

1 Trace over the large cat's head on page 35 on to white paper with a soft pencil; or photocopy the design as many times as required to cover the T-shirt front. For a small T-shirt you will need approximately nine cats' heads.

2 Using scissors or a craft knife and a cutting mat, carefully cut around each cat's head. Cut around the feature lines, removing the eyes, nose, mouth and inner ears.

3 Arrange the paper heads on the T-shirt front, securing firmly in place with double sided tape.

4 Hand tear strips of masking tape to between 5-7.5cm (2-3in) in length and in a variety of shapes. Place them in an interesting pattern on the T-shirt front, between the cats' heads.

Preparing the T-shirt

1 Cut a piece of white cardboard the same size as the T-shirt front. Position inside the T-shirt - this will prevent the paint from bleeding on to the fabric beneath. The card will also keep the surface material flat.

2 Cover your working surface with clean paper or a sheet.

Applying the paint

1 As this is a reversed stencil design, the cats' heads and the fabric where you have stuck the torn masking tape strips will be unpainted: the background fabric will be stencilled in paint tones from light through to dark pink and from light to dark blue and mauve. On a flat dish mix a quantity of paint: red and white in varying proportions to make light/dark pink and blue and white to make light/dark blue and mauve.

2 Practice applying the paint to a scrap of T-shirt fabric until you feel confident with the spread and texture of the paint. Using a large stencil brush, lightly stipple the paint around the cat motifs and torn tape strips. Continue changing colours and apply the paint over the background of the T-shirt, cleaning the brush in water and drying between colours. Use dark/light blue in the bottom right corner of the T-shirt and light mauve in the top left; in the middle use light/dark pink.

3 Using a small stencil brush, paint the eyes in shades of blue or green and the noses in pink. Change to a small watercolour brush and paint the mouth and ear detail in pink.

4 Allow the paint to dry before removing the cat motifs and masking tape strips.

5 Using the watercolour brush freehand, paint the pupils black and white and the whiskers silver. When completely dry remove the card insert.

Fixing the design

1 To fix the paint: cover the design with a white cotton cloth and iron using a cotton setting. The T-shirt can then be hand-washed and dried flat.

Painting the sneakers

1 Remove the laces from the sneakers and stuff with tissue paper to form a firm base. Cover the rubber on the sides of the sneakers with masking tape to prevent paint splashes.

2 Following the instructions for the T-shirt, prepare a number of cats' head traces - you will need approximately one medium and eight small for each adult sneaker and one small for each child's sneaker. You will also need a number of torn masking tape strips.

3 Arrange the heads and the torn strips on the sneakers and secure with double sided tape.

4 Stipple paint on to the sneakers in the same way as the T-shirt, completing the finer facial details with the watercolour brush.

5 Cover with a white cotton cloth and fix with a hot iron, taking care not to melt the rubber soles.

6 The laces can also be painted and fixed by ironing in the same way as the sneakers.

Trace or photocopy these cat motifs and cut out to create your reversed stencil design.

Folk Art Kitchen Set

These simple motifs are ideal for using on wooden utensils or plain furniture, reflecting a folk-art style of design. The pastel shades mixed with warm terracotta, blend easily with modern kitchen designs and colours

If you are using an old wooden tray to complete this project: sand down thoroughly, before applying the base coats of paint.

You will need

- Wooden tray – 41x25cm (16x10in)
- Utensil holder
- Wooden box
- Acrylic paint – cream, yellow, terracotta, green, blue
- Sponge
- Stencil card, film or acetate
- Typewriter carbon paper, white paper, ball-point pen, soft pencil
- Masking tape, metal ruler or straight edge
- Matt acrylic varnish, decorator's paint brush
- Craft knife, cutting mat, fine sandpaper
- Flat dish for mixing paint, container of clean water, kitchen paper

Tracing the design

1 As the motifs in this design are repeated several times around the tray and the boxes, it may help when positioning the stencils if they are cut from acetate or stencil film. Trace over the motifs on pages 40 and 41 on to clear film or acetate with a felt-tipped pen (see Making Stencils, page 8). Make the individual stencils following the diagrams on page 39.

2 If you are using stencil card, cut pieces 5cm (2in) larger than each part of the design. Cut the carbon paper to the same size. Lay the stencil card on a flat surface and secure with small pieces of masking tape. Lay the carbon paper on top, inked side facing down. Over this, lay a tracing and fix securely with masking tape. Carefully go over the design lines with ball-point pen, pressing hard enough to ensure a good transfer.

Cutting the stencil

1 Place the stencil card, stencil film or acetate on a cutting mat and hold with one hand. Using a sharp craft knife, ruler or straight edge carefully cut out the design. Start cutting from the centre of the design – this will ensure the stencil structure stays firm (see Making Stencils page 8). Move the stencil around as you cut, drawing the knife towards you. Make sure that you cut cleanly into any corners. If you make a mistake and cut incorrectly, repair

the stencil with sticky tape then cut away any excess tape the knife. For the checkered design cut out each alternate square.

2 Check the underside of the stencil for snags – these should be removed carefully with fine sandpaper.

3 Once all the motifs have been cut out, check their fit. It is important that the stencil lays flat against the surface being stencilled or the paint will creep under the edges: test the stencil then cut away any excess, leaving a border of approximately 2.5cm (1 in) around the design.

Preparing the surfaces

1 Lightly sand the tray, utensils holder and box. Wipe over with a damp cloth to remove any dust or marks. Apply two coats of cream acrylic paint. Paint the box lid with two coats of terracotta. Leave to dry.

Painting the tray

1 Each stencil will have to be used several times over, so use small pieces of masking tape to attach the stencil to the prepared surface.

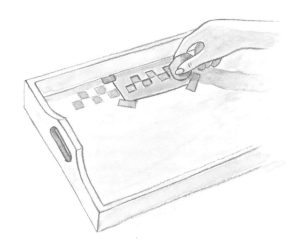

2 Pour green paint into a flat dish. Dip the sponge into the paint. Starting with the checkered border edge, work around the four sides of the tray, applying the paint with the sponge. Leave the paint dry.

3 Position the star shaped stencil in the centre of the tray. Secure with masking tape and sponge the yellow paint on to the tray. Remove the stencil. Leave to dry.

4 Using blue paint stencil the triangles around the star. Finish by stencilling the hearts on to the tray using the terracotta paint.

Painting the holder and box

1 Using blue paint, stencil triangular shapes around the bottom edge of the box. Stencil a small heart in terracotta between each triangle. Leave to dry.

2 Stencil the checkered design in green, around the sides of the utensil box. Leave to dry. Using terracotta paint stencil hearts centrally, on each of the long sides and a small heart at each end. Leave to dry.

Finishing the surfaces

1 When the paint is completely dry, seal with two coats of clear matt acrylic varnish.

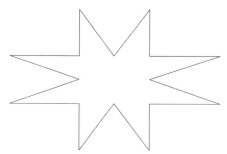

Stage 1 - Yellow Star

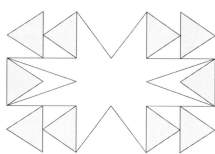

Stage 2 - Blue Triangles

Building up the design

Using the motifs overleaf, cut three separate stencils for the central motif: paint the star shape with yellow paint; the small triangles with blue and the central heart on top of the yellow star with terracotta. Make a checkered border stencil, cutting out alternate squares.

Stage 3 - Terracotta Heart

Triangle Border

Heart

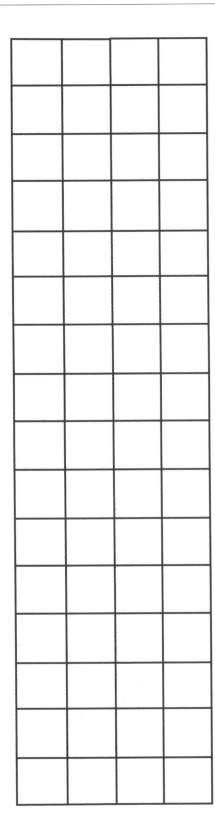

Checkered Border

Use the checkered border; triangle border and heart; and the motifs opposite to cut the stencils for painting your Folk Art Kitchen Set.

Country Style Chicken

This country-style chicken design stencilled on a bread board will make a charming picture to stand on a shelf in the kitchen; or stencil the smaller motifs on cupboard doors, or perhaps on a pine dresser, bringing country charm to your kitchen

NOTE The painted bread board should be used for decorative purposes only.

You will need

- Wooden bread board
- Small wooden cupboard
- Stencil paint – white, black, forest green, brick red, deep blue, buttercup yellow, brown
- Water based brush-on or spray acrylic varnish
- Typewriter carbon paper, white paper, ball-point pen, soft pencil
- Stencil card, film or acetate
- Craft knife, cutting mat, fine sandpaper
- Masking tape, spray mount adhesive, sticky tape
- Small and medium stencil brush, fine paintbrush, flat decorator's paint brush
- Container of clean water, flat dish for mixing paint, kitchen paper, newspaper, soft cloth

Tracing the design

1 Trace over the chicken design on page 47 on to white paper with a soft pencil. Alternatively trace directly on to stencil film or acetate. Lay the tracing over the bread board to check that the design will fit on to the flat area of the board.

2 If you are using stencil card, cut a piece 5cm (2in) larger than the chicken tracing, cut the carbon paper to the same size. Lay the stencil card on a flat surface and secure with small pieces of masking tape. Lay the carbon paper on top, inked side facing down. Over this, lay the chicken tracing; fix securely with masking tape. Carefully go over the design lines with a ball-point pen, pressing hard enough to ensure a good transfer.

Cutting the stencil

1 Place the stencil card, stencil film or acetate on a cutting mat and hold with one hand. Using a sharp craft knife, and following the design lines, start cutting from the centre of the design – this will ensure the stencil structure stays firm (see Making Stencils, page 8). Move the stencil around as you cut, drawing the knife towards you.

2 If you make a mistake and cut incorrectly, repair the stencil with sticky tape then cut away any excess tape with a sharp knife.

3 After the stencil has been cut, check the underside for snags – these should be removed carefully with fine sandpaper.

4 Lay the chicken stencil on the bread board and cut around the design, roughly to the size of the flat area of the board – this will ensure the stencil lies completely flat.

Positioning the stencil

1 Using fine sandpaper, gently sand down the flat area of the bread board to remove any surface varnish. Wipe over the board with a clean soft cloth. If you are using an old bread board, check the surface for cuts, stains or varnish: use sandpaper to rub away any surface marks or remove the varnish before painting.

2 Lay the stencil face down on a piece of newspaper. Finely coat the back of the stencil with spray mount adhesive: the adhesive will hold the stencil firmly while painting, but can easily be removed with a little white spirit.

3 Position the stencil on the bread board, holding firmly in place with small pieces of masking tape.

Painting the bread board

1 Using the medium stencil brush, pick up some of the buttercup yellow paint and apply in a soft pouncing or a gentle circular movement to the body, beak and tail area of the chicken. Make sure that you do not smudge the paint under the edge of the stencil. To remove any excess paint from the brush, dab on kitchen paper at regular intervals. Between colours, clean the stencil brush in clean water (see Washing Brushes, page 11).

2 In a dish, mix together a small amount of red and yellow paint to make orange. Using the small stencil brush, add orange highlights to the edges of the body, beak and tail feathers; add contours to the body shape and legs using brick red.

3 Using the small stencil brush, apply brick red paint mixed with a little black to the chicken's comb and wattle. Use the same dark brick red paint to add highlights to the top side of the tail feathers.

4 Using the small brush, apply forest green to the grass area of the stencil. Lighten or darken the paint with black or white, then using the small brush, add detail to the grass.

5 Apply white paint to the cloud area and chicken's eye. When the paint is dry, highlight the front edges of the comb and wattle using white paint. Mix a very small amount of light and medium blue paint and, using the small brush, carefully apply the paint over the white cloud area.

6 When the paint is dry carefully remove the stencil. Using a fine paintbrush, add a small dot of black to the eye and the beak.

7 To finish the design add a small amount of green paint to the outer section of the bread board. You may be able to follow the edge of the board or there may be a raised section of the design that you can paint.

Painting the cupboard

1 Sand the egg cupboard all over to remove any rough patches of wood. Wipe over with a clean soft cloth. In a dish mix forest green paint with a little white. Dilute with water to make a pale green wash.

2 Brush the colour wash over the whole of the cupboard and leave to dry. This will give a pale coloured base on which the stencil design can be applied (see Hints and Tips, page 13).

3 Cut the egg basket, bluebell and the flower motif stencils, using the outline on page 46 and 47. Position the basket stencil on to the front of the cupboard.

4 In a dish mix together a little brick red and buttercup yellow paint, to make a terracotta colour. Using a small stencil brush, apply the mixed paint to the basket and handle area of the design; on top add highlights using the brick red paint.

5 Using the small brush, apply brown to the eggs; highlight the tops with brown, mixed with a little white. As you are working in a very small area, take care not to smudge the paint. If you are worried about this, wait until the basket has dried before continuing. Using the small paintbrush, apply forest green paint to the grass area under the basket. When all the paint is dry remove the stencil.

6 Attach the bluebell stencil to the side of the box with small pieces of masking tape. Mix forest green with white to make a light green. Using the small brush, apply light green to the flower stems and deep blue highlighted with white to the bluebells. When the paint is dry carefully remove the stencil, then repeat the process for the other side of the cupboard.

7 Complete the top panel in the same way, using the flower motif. When dry remove the stencil.

8 To finish, stipple the door edge with green paint using the medium brush and add a green painted line to the raised area around the door panel.

Sealing the surfaces

1 The painted areas of the design should be sealed using a matt acrylic varnish: this will help to protect them from dust and knocks. Using a soft cloth, gently wipe the cupboard and bread board to remove any dust particles.

2 If you are using a spray varnish: work in a well ventilated room, covering your working surface with newspaper. Spray using a controlled action, keeping the can moving gently across the project.

3 If you are using brush-on matt acrylic varnish: dip the brush in the varnish and apply evenly to the surface of the project. Make sure that you brush out runs and that you finish off painting in the same direction as the grain of the wood. Build up two or three coats of varnish.

Use these design motifs to cut your chicken, flower and egg basket stencils.

Egg Basket

Flower Motif

Chicken

Top

Bluebell

Ivy Leaf Christmas

Ivy is almost as important to the Christmas festivities as crackers or mince pies. For centuries this evergreen has been used to decorate homes for the holidays. Although real ivy has been used to make the stencils, we have included a leaf trace so that you won't have to brave the cold to complete the project

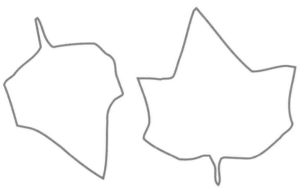

You will need

- For the cake band and placemat: white Aida band, cross stitch fabric — the height of the cake x the distance around, adding extra for overlapping; the height of the placemat, adding extra for turnings top and bottom
- For the napkin: white aida napkin, lace trimmed
- Real ivy leaves
- Fabric paint — dark, ivy and light green, gold, red
- Thin cork sheet, felt-tipped pen
- Craft knife, small scissors, cutting mat
- Small stencil brush, paint brush, masking tape
- Container of clean water, flat dish for mixing paint, kitchen paper
- Iron, fluffy towel

Cutting the stencil

1 Using masking tape stick an ivy leaf on to a piece of thin cork sheet. Draw around the leaf shape with a felt-tipped pen.

2 Place the cork on a cutting mat and using a craft knife or small scissors, cut around the shape (see Making a Leaf Stencil, page 9).

Painting the leaf

1 Stretch the strips of Aida band and the napkin on a flat, paper covered surface.

2 Load a stencil brush with ivy green paint, (see Painting Techniques, page 10). Hold the leaf stencil on to the fabric, and with an almost dry brush, pounce on to the fabric. Add the light green and gold paint in the same way. Remove the stencil, wipe, then reposition.

3 With dark green paint, and using the blunt end of a paint brush, add veins and stalks to each leaf.

4 For the berries: load the stencil brush with red paint. Place the end of the bristles flat on the fabric, then twist clockwise transferring the paint to the fabric. Leave flat to dry.

5 Place the fabric face down on a towel and iron for 1-2 minutes to fix the paint (see Fixing Fabric Paint, page 12).

Geometric Rug

Reminiscent of Mexican folk-art, these simple motifs and colours combine with the natural texture of the rug to create a traditionally inspired, yet up-to-date style. For an inexpensive yet co-ordinated look why not use the rug as a wall hanging and repeat the motifs on a tablecloth or lampshade

Buy a rug that can be hand or machine washed: after painting the rug can be sealed with PVA glue – this will help protect the design and permit careful hand washing.

You will need

- Plain woven rug – beige
- Emulsion paint – red, pale blue, ochre, yellow, deep blue
- Stencil card, film or acetate, craft knife, cutting mat, fine sandpaper
- Typewriter carbon paper, white paper, ball-point pen, soft pencil
- Small stencil brushes or small stiff brushes, masking tape, flat dish for mixing paint
- Newspaper, PVA glue, container of clean water, decorator's brush, kitchen paper

Making the stencil

1 Trace over the geometric shapes on pages 53, 54 and 55 on to white paper with a soft pencil. Alternatively trace directly on to stencil film or acetate (see Making Stencils, page 8).

2 If you are using stencil card, cut pieces 5cm (2in) larger than each geometric shape. Cut the carbon paper to the same size. Lay the stencil card on a flat surface with the carbon paper, inked side facing down, on top. Over this, lay a geometric tracing and fix securely with masking tape. Carefully go over the design lines with a ball-point pen, pressing hard enough to ensure a good transfer.

3 Place the stencil card, film or acetate on to a cutting mat and using a craft knife, cut out the stencil (see Making Stencils, page 8).

Preparing the rug

1 Lay the rug on a flat work table or on the floor. Make sure the area is clean and uncluttered.

2 Decide, depending on the size and shape of your rug, how much of the design you will use and how the shapes will be positioned: whether to do strips of the border design from one side to the other, or if to be more ambitious and take the design down the sides and around the corners.

3 Mark lightly with a soft pencil the centre of the rug and the point where each section of the design will be positioned. If a border is going around the rug it is a good idea to start in the middle of a long side and work both ways until you get to the corner. If the design will not logically go round a corner, a gap can be left between the end of one side and the beginning of the next. This can be filled with another small design, a triangle or a small part of the central medallion for example.

Painting the rug

1 Decide on the various colours of emulsion paint to be used. Cover your working area with newspaper: keep kitchen roll, masking tape and the stencil brushes close at hand. Try out the colours on paper before starting on the rug.

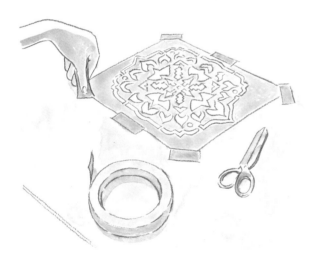

2 Put a teaspoon of each colour paint on a flat dish or on the lid of each tin. Place the central medallion on the rug: line up the centre of the stencil with the centre of the rug. Hold in place with masking tape: after a while you may find you can work without fixing the stencil. Which ever method you choose: the stencil must be a flat on the surface of the rug.

3 Using the small stencil brush, pick up some of the first paint colour you are using. Dab off most of the paint on to the newspaper leaving the brush almost 'dry'. When stencilling on to fabric it is far better to have too little paint on the brush than too much.

4 Apply the paint in a soft pouncing or a gentle circular motion, holding the stencil flat on the surface of the rug. Work the paint into the fabric: build up the colour slowly without applying too much paint. If you are using different colours close to one another on a stencil, it may help to use a smaller brush; or mask off the part of the stencil that is to be painted in a different colour. Use a different brush for each colour: store each brush, when not in use, with its own coloured pot of paint – this way you will avoid picking up the wrong colour on the wrong brush. If you have to wash a stencil brush, make sure it is completely dry before using it again.

5 As there will be a large area of wet paint, great care should be taken when removing and re-positioning the stencils. Peel the stencil carefully from the rug, wipe away any paint marks, before re-positioning over the next area to be painted.

Sealing the surface

6 When the stencilling is finished, leave the rug flat to dry overnight. Mix PVA glue with an equal quantity of water. Using a flat decorator's brush, paint over the top surface of the rug, working the mix down into the weave of the fabric. Make sure all the stencilled parts are completely covered with the glue. Leave the rug flat to dry for several days. The glue will seal the surface of the rug and allow marks to be wiped from the surface (see Painting on Fabric, page 12).

Use these designs to cut the stencils for painting your rug. Follow the photograph above for positioning the stencils on the fabric.

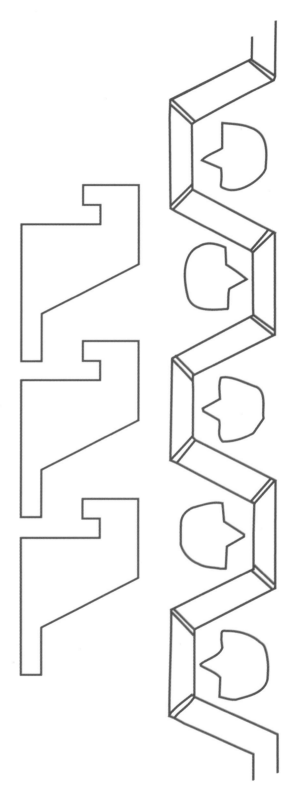

Border Motifs

Border Motifs

Border Motifs

Central Medallion

Vegetable Trug and Apron

Cutting fresh vegetables is a true pleasure, nothing tastes quite
like garden produce harvested on the day it will be eaten. This
charming trug is the ideal way to collect your precious vegetables,
and the pretty apron will keep the soil off your Sunday best!

You will need

- Wooden trug
- Cotton or calico apron
- Acrylic paint – ultramarine blue, cadnium yellow, black, lemon, crimson, bright green
- Emulsion paint – white
- Fabric paint – pale blue, yellow, black, red
- Acrylic drying retarder
- Water based brush-on matt acrylic varnish
- Stencil card, film or acetate
- Typewriter carbon paper, white paper, ball-point pen, soft pencil, ruler
- Craft knife, cutting mat, fine sandpaper
- Masking tape 3.5cm (1³⁄₈in) wide, spray mount adhesive, pins
- Cardboard, lining paper
- Small and medium stencil brush, decorator's paint brush, natural sponge (small pieces)
- Flat dish for mixing paint, container of clean water, kitchen paper, newspaper, soft cloth, cocktail stick, rubber band
- Iron, clean cloth

Tracing the design

1 Trace over the vegetable motifs on page 61 on to white paper with a soft pencil. Alternatively trace directly on to stencil film or acetate (see Making Stencils, page 8).

2 If you are using stencil card, cut pieces 5cm (2in) larger than each vegetable, and a piece large enough to take several leaves. Cut the carbon paper to the same size. Lay the stencil card on a flat surface and secure with small pieces of masking tape. Lay the carbon paper on top, inked side facing down. Over this, lay a vegetable tracing and fix securely with masking tape. Carefully go over the design lines with a ball-point pen, pressing hard enough to ensure a good transfer.

Cutting the stencil

1 Place the stencil card, stencil film or acetate on a cutting mat and hold with one hand. Using a sharp craft knife, and following the design lines, start cutting from the centre of the design – this will ensure the stencil structure stays firm (see Making Stencils, page 8). Move the stencil around as you cut, drawing the knife towards you. Make sure that you cut cleanly into any corners. If you make a mistake and cut incorrectly, repair the stencil with sticky tape then cut away any excess tape with a sharp knife. Carefully remove any snags on the underside with fine sandpaper.

2 Once all the vegetable stencils have been cut out, check their fit. It is important that the stencil lays flat against the surface being stencilled or the paint will creep under the edges: test the stencil against the trug then cut away any excess, leaving a border of about 2.5cm (1 in) around each stencil design.

Preparing the surface

1 Lightly sand the trug to remove any rough edges. Wipe over with a damp cloth to remove any dust or marks.

2 Mix a small amount of white emulsion paint in water. Using a paint brush, test the wash on the underside of the trug: if the colour is too pale, add more paint to the mix. Paint the wash over the entire surface of the trug. Leave to dry completely – this may take several days.

Positioning the stencil

1 Lay the stencils face down on a piece of newspaper. In a well ventilated room, finely coat the back of each with spray mount adhesive: the adhesive will hold the stencil firmly while painting, but can easily be removed from the stencil and the wood with a little white spirit on a soft cloth.

2 Position each stencil on the trug, holding firmly in place with small pieces of masking tape.

Painting the carrot

1 When applying paint it is easier to start with a light colour, adding paint to deepen the colour. Acrylic paint dries very quickly so it is advisable to mix small quantities of paint and to add a drying retarder to the paint. This will not affect the colour but will allow you more time to apply the paint. Follow the manufacturer's instructions regarding the proportion of paint to retarder but it is usually equivalent to a third of the amount of paint. It is most important to thoroughly wash and dry the brush and sponge between colours (see Washing Brushes, page 11).

2 Squeeze out a small amount of crimson and cadnium yellow acrylic paint on to a flat dish. Using a cocktail stick, gradually blend the crimson into the yellow until you have a deep orange colour. To this add a small amount of paint retarder.

3 Pick up the little of the colour on your stencil brush, remove any excess on a piece of kitchen paper, then apply to the carrot in a gentle pouncing, circular movement. As the stencil is curved over the side of the trug, take care not to lift the edges of the stencil as you apply the paint.

4 With a cocktail stick, mix a little more red with the orange paint. Dab on to the edges of the carrot, using a small piece of sponge that has been softened in water and thoroughly dried on kitchen paper.

5 Squeeze a little bright green paint on to the mixing dish. Dip the sponge in to the paint, then dab on to the stalks of the carrot.

6 To fill the sides of the trug, each vegetable will need to be stencilled more than once. Remove the stencil carefully, clean off any wet paint (see Cleaning a Stencil, page 11) and re-position on the trug.

Painting the cabbage

1 Squeeze out a small amount of ultramarine blue and a larger amount of cadnium yellow. Slowly add the blue to the yellow until it turns light green, then add the retarder. Using a stencil brush, apply to the cabbage stencil.

2 Add more blue to a small amount of the light green mix – this will deepen the green. Apply using a piece of sponge to the leaves, darkening the colour as it radiates out towards the outer leaves.

3 Finally, to the dark green mix add a tiny amount of black, which is sponged on the edges of the cabbage leaves. Remove the stencil and re-position.

Painting the beetroot

1 Squeeze out a small amount of black with a larger amount of the crimson. Very carefully, using a cocktail stick, add the black to the crimson until the colour turns to a plum red, then add retarder. Using a stencil brush apply to the beetroot stencil.

2 To add shading to the beetroot, taking a small amount of the plum red to one side add more black to produce a deeper plum colour. Using a piece of sponge apply the paint to the beetroot. Remove stencil and repeat.

Painting the peas

1 Squeeze out a little ultramarine blue with a larger amount of lemon. Mix blue with the lemon to produce a leafy green, then add retarder. Apply with a stencil brush over the whole of the stencil.

2 Mix a little of the leafy green paint with blue to produce a deeper green. Apply to the peas with a sponge.

3 Using another piece of sponge carefully apply a tiny amount of the cadmium yellow to each of the peas. Remove the stencil and re-position.

Painting the handle

1 Coat the back of the leaf stencil with spray mount, then position on the trug handle.

2 Apply bright green paint to the leaves using a small piece of sponge.

3 Add a little ultramarine blue to the green paint to give a darker green and sponge lightly over the leaves to give a two tone effect.

4 Re-position the stencil and repeat down the length of the handle.

5 When the paint is completely dry, seal the surface with two coats of matt acrylic varnish.

Stencilling the apron

1 Lay the apron on a clean surface and mark the centre line with pins. Place a strip of masking tape down the centre of the apron, remove the pins. Avoid the pocket area as this will be stencilled later.

2 Measure 2.5cm (1in) from the side of the masking tape and mark with a pin. Do this several times down the length of the apron. Place a second strip of masking tape beside the pins. Continue taping strips until you have covered the surface of the apron.

3 Place a piece of cardboard inside the pocket to prevent the stencil paint bleeding through to the apron fabric.

Applying the stencil

1 Cover the table with lining paper. Lay the apron on the paper and fix firmly in place with masking tape.

2 Spray the reverse side of the leaf stencil with spray mount. When tacky, position at the top of the apron, between the masking tape strips.

3 Mix a yellow fabric paint with pale blue until you have a bright green. Test the colour on a spare piece of fabric before starting.

4 Wrap a rubber band around the stencil brush to hold the bristles firmly in place. Dab the paint on to the leaf stencil, taking care not to allow the paint on to any other areas of the fabric. Do not load the brush with too much paint or it will smudge when you remove the stencil.

5 Allow each area to dry for a few minutes before removing the stencil and moving it further down the strip. Continue across the whole of the apron.

6 Position the vegetable stencils on to the apron pocket.

7 Mix the fabric paints to the same colours used on the trug. Apply to the pocket area with a sponge.

Fixing the paint

1 When completely dry, remove the masking tape strips and the cardboard from the pocket.

2 Cover the stencilled areas of the apron with a piece of cotton fabric and iron on a cotton setting to fix the paint (see Fixing Fabric Paint, page 12).

Cut your vegetable stencils using these templates, the small leaf repeats on the handle of the trug and in strips down the apron.

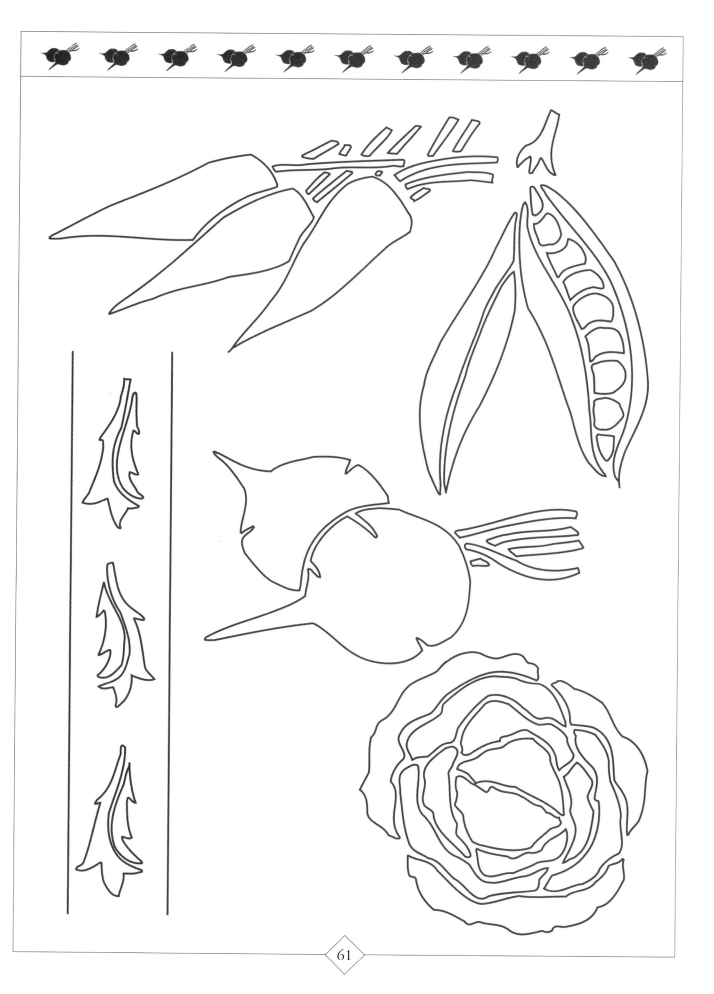

Acknowledgements

Thanks to the designers for contributing such wonderful projects:
Barge Roses Garden Set (page 14), Amanda Davidson
Scribble Bag and Box (page 20), Cheryl Owen
Lacy Wrapping and Cards (page 24), Cheryl Owen
Farmyard Tiles (page 28), Susan Penny
Cat T-shirt and Sneakers (page 32), Amanda Davidson
Folk Art Kitchen Set (page 36), Janet Bridge
Country Style Chicken (page 42), Sarah Gibb
Ivy Leaf Christmas (page 48), Susan Penny
Geometric Rug (page 50), Kate Fox
Vegetable Trug and Apron (page 56), Lynn Strange

Many thanks to Ashton James and Jon Stone for their inspirational photography;
DMC for supplying material for the projects; Lakeland Limited for supplying kitchen
equipment and Chris Strange for supplying fresh produce for use in photography.

Other books in the Made Easy series

Stamping (David & Charles, 1998)

Glass Painting (David & Charles, 1998)

Silk Painting (David & Charles, 1998)